THE
KAIROS EFFECT

THE KAIROS EFFECT

A biological approach to social problems

Carl Jenkins, M.D.

MEDICAL PLACE PUBLISHERS
SPRINGFIELD, OHIO

Published by Medical Place Publishers
2055 S. Limestone Street, Springfield, Ohio 45505

Publisher's Cataloging-in-Publication Data
Jenkins, Carl.
   The kairos effect: a biological approach to social problems /
   Carl Jenkins ; Springfield, Ohio : Medical Place Publishers, 1997.
      p.   ill.   cm.
   Includes bibliographical references and index.
   ISBN 0-9656818-0-7
   1. Sociobiology. 2. Race relations.   3. Social problems. I. Title.
GN365.9.J46   1997
304'.5   dc—21   97-65080

Illustrations by Herbert K. Skinner, Jr.

PROJECT COORDINATION BY JENKINS GROUP

00 99 98   ◈   5 4 3 2 1

Printed in the United States of America

To the human race

WHY DID BLACK PEOPLE IN ST. PETERSBURG, FLORIDA, burn down their houses, loot what seemed to be their own stores, and shoot and turn over cars passing through their area?

Why did the departing Croatians burn their houses before leaving them vacant for new inhabitants to establish their land claims?

Dr. Carl Jenkins, a medical professor, explains this behavior with his theory of "human animal territorialism." Drawing on well-known theories of human behavior, Jenkins makes a persuasive case that racism and acts of aggression are based more on human genetic programming to defend and preserve territory rather than deeply felt hatred.

Jenkins' work carries huge implications for policy makers. He suggests, for example, that ghettos of government housing exacerbate the problem of territorialism, causing far more problems than they solve.

Dr. Jenkins' theory and proposed solutions will surely meet with controversy. But certainly, his ideas present a refreshing angle to solving stubborn societal problems, both in the United States and globally.

CONTENTS

Illustrations by Herbert K. Skinner, Jr.

FOREWORD

THE TIME HAS COME TO TRY TO EVALUATE HUMAN REAC-
tion via computer programming. In order to accomplish
this, however, there is a necessity to have at least some
basis of thought progression which evolved in the following manner:

"T-Factor" (Territorial Factor), the absolute uncon-
trolled link between our genetic background and territory, is the result of personal thought beginning prior to
1968. It was about that time I began to realize current
theories regarding racial problems were not valid explanations that could be supported by substantial evidence.

These thoughts resulted in a thesis called "Human
Animal Territorialism" (HAT), which I presented at a
National Medical Association meeting in San Francisco,

California, in August 1969. Simply stated, my conclusion was that the controlling power in a territory (whomever wears the HAT) determines the level of racism. (Printed in *Journal of Human Relations*, 1969, Central State University.) My ideas were heavily influenced by the works of Konrad Z. Lorenz, Desmond Morris, and Sidney Aronson. I applied some of their consideration to human problems.

To further share ideas, I then wrote and published "Human Animal Territorialism," a manual for college discussion; and "We are all Lions," a manual which explains racial problems, by means of illustrations, to children from five to twelve years of age.

Other activities intervened, and my writing was temporarily interrupted. But over and over again, throughout the years, I saw the basic idea of territorialism at work—camouflaged and unrecognized—in man's affairs. Not only did it appear to influence racial problems, but also religious differences, and male-female relationships, with conclusions evident at all levels of government. I now feel an urgency to again focus attention on this fundamental rule of nature.

Some common applications are in the areas of religion, male-female relationships, government planning, and inner-city problems; as well as racial tensions. These interface with a common denominator, the "T-Factor," in a summation of thoughts and writings of many authorities, with conclusions of my own.

Like the original thesis, the HAT term is used to bring to the reader the realization that this is a human animal imperative.

The term "animal" is used to remind readers that we are only a single or multiple chromosome apart from other living creatures. Lion illustrations are used to reinforce this idea.

"T-Factor" is the proposed basic chromosomal cell component driving force, not yet placed in the genetic chain. It is apparent and needs recognition at this time, the "Kairos" moment, the appropriate time to grasp its impact. "Territorial factor" is a term used for measuring the absolute link between our genetic development and land or environment.

Mankind will come to realize that we are forcefully controlled by inherited factors. As we comprehend this, we can begin to manipulate natural forces to form a more serene and tranquil environment—if we want.

PREFACE

I SAT IN THE MORNING DAYLIGHT, LIKE A ROBIN BEATING at the window, searching for an answer to the mystery of what lies beyond the glass. Driving home slowly, my mind was focused upon the fact that nothing from research, nor my own knowledge from life's experiences, fully explained the unrest that seemed to encompass so many areas of life.

Like a robin, I felt there was an answer on the other side of the glass. This particular morning, there was silence inside the automobile, an eerie blackness, with my thoughts searching through billions of impulses.

Suddenly, as though someone had opened the window, I had a clear, undistorted view. I knew the answer: genetic programming—human animal territorialism.

ACKNOWLEDGMENTS

Many people have contributed to make this dream of mine a reality. I wish to thank my office staff, for their generous support and assistance. Thank you: Sonya, Katheryn, Dena, Cindi, and especially Angela.

To my many friends who supported my efforts, I am indebted. My gratitude extends to those acquaintances who became friends, through shared efforts during my journey into publication. I am truly grateful to each and every one of you!

Over all, I thank Judy, my companion, who understood everything and sustained me.

As my thoughts progressed from "Hat," to "Human Animal Territorialism," to "We Are All Lions," to "Race and Virtual Reality," and to "Kairos," multiple suggestions and criticisms came from many areas and backgrounds: Sister Jacqueline Studer, R.S.M.; Pastor Richard McDaniel; Father Marvin Hackman; Sally Abbott, M.D.; Mary Ellen Jones, Ph.D.; Mier Bizer, M.D.; Police Chief Roger Evans; Sheriff's Sergeant Sherry Elliott; author and Republican Activist, Elaine B. Jenkins (no relation); artist Herbert Skinner; developer Jack Smart, Jr.; State Senator Rhine McLin; Lowell Schleicher, an inventor and scientist; and biologist Charles Shaffer, Ph.D.

I owe other people who "didn't understand" or suggested I "make it simpler." I am hugely indebted to the multitude of writers on racial problems, who said nothing, and usually concluded with "we must." They forced me to come forth with a more valid approach to bypass conventional thinking.

And, finally, to Reverend Martin Luther King, Jr., when he said on April 3, 1968, "I have been to the mountain top and I've seen the Promised Land." This meant more than even he realized.

INTRODUCTION

I ASK YOU TO FORGET EVERYTHING YOU THOUGHT YOU KNEW about world relations and social unrest, and to form new opinions based on the following outlined principles. Suppose that you and I could come to some sort of conclusion or possible solution to problems which have plagued our communities for as long as either of us care to remember? Let's find a simple, uncomplicated theory—and try it!

All males-females, Islamics-Christians-Jews, Serbs-Muslims, Hutus-Tutsis, North Koreans-South Koreans, Iranians-Iraquians, Blacks-Whites-Hispanics-Orientals, etc., have one thing in common: they are born with their genetic make-up already intact due to a microscopic material called DNA. DNA is not a new topic of discussion;

however, I will focus on the fact that DNA has significant influence on how every one of us reacts to what we perceive as a threat to our survival.

The idea is that the real competition between groups stems from a lack (real or imagined) of adequate resources to supply the demand they create, or to demand resources from others who have too much or too little. In order to do this, they must control land, which is everything.

The DNA which drives territoriality has been manipulating us all along! In the United States we have managed to contain territoriality control to some degree. For instance, we have changed rules to enable females to own land, to vote, to compete in sports, and to enjoy careers that were once available only to males. We try democratic racial approaches, we allow freedom of speech and freedom of religious beliefs and practices, and we give our support, whenever possible, to those countries which are still fighting to accomplish these goals.

Let's rethink the cause-and-effect principle. A person's skin color or ethnic background would hardly seem just *cause* to provoke the *effect* of racial or other violence from otherwise peaceful human beings. A more believable *cause* might be the competition (real or imagined) for less plentiful resources to be shared among the population. Anything from an individual drink of water or a bite of food, to an entire nation's water, food, or fuel supply could be a just *cause*. Now you're beginning to understand!

Forget everything you thought you knew about race relations and start over. Because it's not now, and never was, what you think or what you thought.

Add on male-female, Islamic-Christian-Jewish, Serb-Muslim, and Hutus-Tutsis. On top, dump North Korea and South Korea, Iran and Iraq, Russia and the U.S., and you get a handle on one thing—you and the world have been wrong all the time. Vietnam should have made you think, but you didn't. You thought you were fighting for a principle. You were. You made it up. You were a sucker all the time!

The DNA that drives territoriality has been laughing at us since time, well, since the beginning. He/she/it says "gimme the land" and you can rule the world, or at least as far as you can see with or without glasses or satellites or whatever.

Make the rules so that females can't own land, can't vote, can't drive cars, can't compete in the marketplace, because they are in for land competition, like minorities, foreigners, and next door neighbors.

Make the rules so that Muslims or Hutus or Jews or Palestinians can't own land and then get them where it hurts.

Make the rules so that untrained and uneducated

minorities have free food, resources, and medical care. They only have to compete for drugs, and they can't buy land.

Make the rules so that political battles escalate into horrendous and massive suicide pacts. Base it all on Identification Manifestation (I.M.). So,

> If you look different
> If you talk different
> If you eat different
> If you smell different
> If you walk different,

and have no land, you don't belong—and every other person carrying DNA-propelled organisms will reject you over and under the table. You don't belong.

The sooner we recognize this DNA programming, we can move forward into the world and re-program our computers. Right?

Kairos

All man can know
is how to respond to the unconditioned
at each moment of decision.

V.A. DEMANT,
RELIGIOUS PROSPECT VIII

THE
KAIROS EFFECT

Boxed In

One

GENETICS, ET CETERA, ET CETERA

IT WAS AN UNEASY TIME IN LOS ANGELES AND DETROIT, along with a myriad of other small towns and large cities. In 1950, in Springfield, Ohio, a Catholic hospital opened with enthusiastic support and funding from the old midwestern city. It designated "white" beds and "black" beds. After newspaper publicity forced it to finally integrate, the administrator sobbed at the admission of racial integration. A myriad of lawsuits, and threats of lawsuits, opened restaurants and clubs across the country, as local heroes put their lifestyles on the line. Martin Luther King, Jr. came with his fellow marchers—Andrew Young, Jesse Jackson, Benjamin Hooks, and others. I was an uncertain reference person, a community leader who raised unanswered questions behind the scenes. Questions such as "What is racism?", "How do we quantitate it?", "How do we tell what is 'worse or better' and what works or doesn't?", and "Why are there so many problems with housing?" I had tried to give in the army. I volunteered my life to a nation which obviously didn't want it, and I asked for answers. Dr. William Banner, a field representative for the National Urban League, finally complained that I asked too many questions with no answers. "You write it—it's your problem," he said.

And that's how Human Animal Territorialism (HAT) was born: as an answer to much more. Now it's time to play the game—to know the rules, to predict the answers in social relationships between the sexes, religions, and ethnic groups—and to use these answers to our advantage. To know when and how.

Knowing the rules enables us to assess "What To Do and How To Do It" (see Chapter Six), if we want to!

A litany of suggested reading follows the text. In general, books, manuals, and papers were read or referred to for many years after the original HAT. Since this text is for general reading, most of these materials can be found in the bibliography. These materials will give the reader many hours of introduction into the wonderful world of how nature directs our survival, and how culture, religion, and sex interact. Later we will talk of programming territorial manifestation.

We now have computers which mimic reality and can be manipulated to extend our thoughts and some senses. Crude perhaps, but when we react to and become a part of decision-making, reaction is measurable. This measurement can be by "interactive virtual reality" and will form the basis of discussion in later chapters. We now have a mushrooming practical reality, and we can program a virtual real-life situation of a seemingly social territorial problem. Then we can forecast, measure, and direct desired results.

Let us consider lifestyle. It can be approached biochemically, with a gene or enzyme approach. Lifestyle can also be defined as territory motivation to protect food supply (job) or increased and preferential sexual activity to provide descendants of the property owner. Territoriality (property ownership) can guarantee nutrition (food) for its owner, with very limited physical expenditure, since the owner can shelter the results of his energy. Thus, families can be contained, offspring protected, multiplied, or advanced. Various authors note when food is scarce or limited, owners leave and feed elsewhere, but keep returning at intervals to announce ownership and evict intruders. Consideration and research of varied authors seems to indicate that at intermediate levels of food abundance, owners stay on their territory and evict the invaders.

As food increases, owners begin to share territory with an invader (at cost to owner because invaders deplete food supply). This brings some benefit: the invaders help with defense (work). Owners tolerate an invader only when benefits of help and defense outweigh the cost of sharing. When food levels drop below the feeding rate, the invaders are evicted from the territory, if possible.

At very high levels of food abundance, the owners abandon all defense—there is no benefit from evicting intruders. Note the lax control of immigration at the Mexican border, or the absorption of West Germany by East Germany.

Today, with the increasing social cost of food, medical care, and job support, immigration control and West German absorption are both in difficulty. Local citizens are rebelling and governmental agencies are checking documentation. Citizens are rebelling at the cost of medical and social support for both legal and illegal immigrants. With this start on a practical recognition of how we are programmed, then we can forecast our reaction singly and in groups. We can modify action extension to suit the occasion. In other words, the most powerful person or group in relation to land (whoever wears the HAT) controls the territory and can direct response.

After considering parameters that we now know or believe, and the liabilities and boundaries of known science, I feel a single entry approach—Human Animal Territorialism (man's relationship to land)—is the logical basis for many problems.

This Human Animal Territorialism social activity can be traced from individual male and female groups, national function, and religious organizations, including sub-recognizable groups. It can be manipulated by Identification Manifestation.

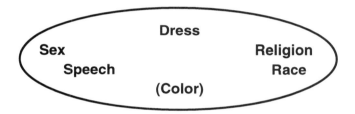

For instance, several years ago, while I was driving at 1:00 a.m. through a local "white" neighborhood, I was stopped by a young policeman and ordered to get out of the car with my hands up. However, his patrol partner soon recognized me, and stopped him by saying, "That's a doctor. He belongs here."

Consideration of the history of slavery recognizes the "T-Factor." The first twenty slaves in this country landed in Jamestown in 1619 and were traded for supplies and materials. As late as 1651, there were no racial problems in the United States.

Former black slaves owned white slaves and had possession of considerable areas of property. Slaves were given free land to settle, intermarried racially, and intermixed without problems. When some black slaves became wealthy and began to own large tracts of land, white landowners looked at their former slaves' prosperity and passed various laws regarding intermarriage and the right to hold property. By contrast, Brazil seemed to have little, if any, racial problems. It was occupied by the Portuguese, whose religious beliefs forbade the breaking up of slave families and allowed slaves to own land. Land possession became a status symbol, finally being sought after by the most status enterprising and the best educated.

We are still naive in our approach to science. On February 5, 1996, *Time* magazine reported that Michael Mayer and Dr. Dedier Quelez of the Geneva Observatory in Switzerland had discovered a new planet, using light spectrometers and computers. Geoffrey Mancy and Paul Butler of San Francisco State University, the article continues, then found a planet six times the mass of Jupiter. It was always there. Our after-the-fact "science" has just evolved to where it can "discover" by combination of sense extenders, in this case telescopes, and spectrometers.

Our grasp of science is superficial. Years ago, Big John Hale, Chief Surgeon of the Meharry Medical School, strode into the medical classroom and announced "I welcome you to the study of the brain." He held aloft the big, thick book that was to crush us with detail, and said "I don't know much about the brain and neither does anyone else." In-depth knowledge of the brain and our world has advanced little since then, even though we have computer pathway responses mimicking brain thought.

Science is after-the-fact and can only be interpreted in present knowledge. Tomorrow may be different. Apples fell before Newton, bacilli and cocci invaded bodies before Lewenholk, and viruses were around before the electron microscope. In 1994, astronomers used the Hubble Space Telescope to find evidence of a huge, black hole in space. In 1996, we discovered that comets produce x-rays. Now we have diseases by prion, an entirely new, just-recognized class and genetic recognition of multiple programmed conditions.

We are just now beginning computer anatomical dissection (with hopes of finding new horizons) and exploring DNA programming reception transport. *Fortune* magazine reported in its November 1, 1993, issue that Victor Spitzer and David Whitlock, of the University of Colorado Health Sciences Center in Denver, were principle investigators of the Visible Human Project, financed by the National Library of Medicine. A thirty-nine year old Texan, who died of an overdose, and a fifty-one year old Maryland female, who died of a heart attack, were available to create the world's first comprehensive digital record of the human body. Thousands of megabytes of data are to be available on CD-ROMS and computer networks. Head-to-toe Magnetic Resonance Imaging (MRI) and Computerized Tomography (CT) scanned the volunteer male and then his body was finalized into twenty-billion bytes and thirty-five CD-ROM disks. They have now started digital recording of this first woman. For every frontier we've crossed, we're not there yet. We are not able to make a single cell. We have really only tried a chemical approach to disease. There must be hundreds of other approaches.

We can attempt to program results from our limited perception. In 1953, Watson & Crick first found and stated an estimate of the chromosomal genetic chain. Since then, we have evolved a composite of genetic strands.

Medicine can now identify bacterial cells addressing genetic traits with different metabolic patterns. We can identify DNA fingerprinting using plasmids, or genetic fingerprinting using all the DNA in a cell. These identify detection on a molecular level. Genetic mutation direction and predisposition, along with assessment, is now clinically used. Each part of our cell is found to correspond in some evolutionary way to our physical makeup.

In March 1996, *Nature* magazine published reports of genetic maps of the human genome, composed entirely of markers known as microsatalites. As we continually inquire, perhaps we will find thought progression, "Kairos" effect soon. Until now, our sense extenders, our computers, physics, and biochemistry were not developed enough to propose and measure behavior; which is what I propose.

History is overflowing with examples of Human Animal Territorialism, but the United States, politically in particular, has failed to reach the apparent conclusion.

England established its great empire characterized by the slogan: "The sun never sets on the British Empire." Soon, however, each of the satellites began their own territorial attachment and grew to challenge their originator.

The United States was one of the first; and Australia, India, Canada, and South Africa followed. Each established its own territoriality and its own identity.

The United States helped win World War II, easily identifying other territorial owners by reason of dress, speech, and other parameters. Problems developed during the Vietnam conflict because United States troops had problems identifying friend and foe, and because this was their land, not ours. This is a lesson which seems to be on the verge of being explained again to the United States—in Somalia, Bosnia, and Korea.

Race identification was easy in Somalia. In spite of our attempts to do token "humanitarian help" by sending in food shipments, we were perceived as not being a part of the territory—a territorial invader. This was promulgated when we used power with local inhabitants, even though our position was that the local inhabitants were affecting the distribution of food regionally. In that situation, we still were assumed to be forcing our will on the territorial owners. Thus we were rejected, even though we believed we were giving "humanitarian help." The more food we gave, the more it looked as if we were invading. When we attempted to protect our supplies, to assure that they were delivered to the needy population, we were the image of an outside invader, therefore an enemy. More and more resistance surfaced, and finally we retired, even though in our own minds, we knew we helped starving Somalians.

In Bosnia, there suddenly seemed to be a newly-emancipated country. Competition was limited for jobs and food supply. Jobs equaled food. Territorial manifestation equaled ownership of food, religious participation, extension of racial guidelines, and sexual preferences. The Croatians, Serbs, and Muslims all have identifiable characteristics. All grasp at territorial ownership in order to extend complete control.

The weaker group, the Muslims, are now pushed down to only ten percent of the territory; and the Croatians, aided temporarily by the Serbs, have driven back the easily-identifiable Muslims. The Dayton agreement, forced by the prospect of an escalation of war between major interested countries, might temporarily halt conflict. It's not difficult to see what will happen, however. The Serbs, Muslims, and Croatians will gradually and continually contest over the remains, until one group can call themselves Bosnians, instead of Serb, Muslim, or Croatian. There will still be homeland conflict.

There is drift in the United States to this extent.

In volume six, number eight of *LEAR* magazine, public television's Charleyne Hunter-Gault said, "I don't think that any intelligent person in America today would seriously set in notion that any group can go its own way in this pleuristic society, and make it. It's just not going to happen; and there's another thing—America is not only pleuristic—it is becoming a mostly brownish, pleuristic country. We can begin to prepare for it, and try to make it as positive an experience as possible; or we can resist it, and end up in the same form as Bosnia, though maybe less terrible." Her idea seemed to be that extensive group separation will lead to severe problems.

"Kairos," identified as being said by V. A. Demant, in Religious Prospect VIII, is defined as: "All man can know is how to respond to the unconditioned at each moment of decision." The time has come to recognize that "unconditioned response" is "T-factor," that chromosomal imperative, and fit it into a framework of modern computer and virtual reality technology.

My use of illustrations reminds the reader that humans are not far from their animal counterpart. In effect "we are all lions." This Identification Manifestation of territorial attachment puts animal reaction in its proper place, one of the prime movers of our social phenomenon. The following chapters will discuss sex, religion, race, and application of the HAT principle (how to identify it, observe it, and make it work for you).

T-Factor

Two

Man-Woman

Territorial Rules

In the jungle, at the base of the Himalayan mountains, the Naga natives wear the HAT. We knew the Japanese were there, but squat Naga Indians strode down to the camp, carrying their poison-tipped arrows behind their shoulders. An Indian interpreter rushed up, talking respectfully. I carried my forty-five lovingly and low.

Our interpreter haltingly explained that the Naga chief, wearing three shrunken heads around his neck, was looking for his lost buffalo. Two walnut-sized and shaped native heads hung from his neck. The third head was Jesse, who had been missing from our camp for three weeks. A guarded question was answered—the heads were two tribal warriors and "a crazy man who came into **our** camp looking for a woman." I agreed. He must have been crazy.

"No buffalo," I said, remembering the tough deer we had eaten a week before. They vanished into the jungle. I caressed my army forty-five. Now we had another problem. A tough deer?

*   *   *   *

Male-Female Territory

MAN-WOMAN

Let us look at territory as it applies to our most common relationship.

Woman is really a slave when she does not control land (territory) and when man keeps her that way. She is an identifiable person representing an inadequate territorial habitat.

In many developed nations today, women are considered to be co-partners. They have vested interests of their own and control a huge portion of wealth in their own names. However—wealth is not necessarily control of land.

In other words, a man-woman relationship may be operable or related to the possession of territory. It is mostly man (men) who holds the land, assets, and money. It is he who rules woman (women) without land, assets or money. Thus, males can hold females in servitude. Man usually can contrive this but in a species who invented sudden stop mechanisms for other animals, there is no reason why this example cannot work the other way. That is, if the generally assumed "weaker sex" could take over the territory, the whole process would be reversed.

For that matter, in a 1995 January/February *Health* magazine under "Fitness," Laura Hilgers noted that women are starting to pull alongside men in Olympic contests. She explained women's unprecedented recent gains in corporate and political life as: "They are finally getting their chance."

Women have had a terrible time claiming their right to territory, even in the United States. Generally mandated as a possession in some cultures, they have been burned and buried at the time of their "master's" death, along with his other possessions. In Kabul, Afghanistan, they have again recently been demoted to an invisible status, supposedly in the name of religion, but really signifying territorial loss.

Equal rights for American women first surfaced after American women were excluded from the World Anti-Slavery Conference in London (1840). A Women's Convention in 1848 proclaimed, "We hold these truths to be self-evident, that all men and women are created equal."

The nineteenth amendment, giving women the right to vote only passed into law in 1920 but the Voting Rights Act, Title VII, banning sexual discrimination was not implemented until 1965.

In December 1993, female workers in Japan's Honda plant, one of the leading automotive plants in the world, were still not allowed on the assembly line with males, and they had to pass by male workers via a tunnel. Females were not allowed in the same cafeteria as males.

Another example of males demanding control was

made public in April 1996, when the Equal Opportunity Commission in Illinois alleged managerial males condoned female harassment in a large auto plant.

Some indicators of territory priority are little noticed. *Health* magazine reported in their November/December 1993 issue that television commentators identified professional male tennis players by their first names only eight percent of the time, while fifty-three percent of the time they identified professional females by their first names.

In April 1996, in an Ohio psychiatric clinic of nine physicians, Dr. Lynn Farney, a female, noted that the six male physicians were always addressed as "Doctor," while the female physicians were often called by their first names.

In 1995, in a well-publicized trial of a husband and wife, the husband was accused of repeatedly beating and raping his wife; and she was accused of retaliating by mutilating her husband. The outcome was predictable— the husband was found not guilty and released, while the wife was found guilty by reason of temporary insanity and sentenced to undergo observation at a mental facility.

Some studies indicate that therapists, even at the simplest level of listening, do not pay attention to women's problems in the way in which they attend to men's. (Dr.

M. J. Hubbard—*Woman, The Misunderstood Majority*) Perhaps this is generally based on a power structure where women are weaker. In reality however, it relates to land control. Dr. Hubbard made other statements, such as when women's sense of self and sense of achievement are relationally based they are therefore inferior.

She listed nineteen misbeliefs under that category, all of which seem to structure subservient "good woman." Dr. Hubbard also quoted historian Barbara Welter: "Women could be divided into four cardinal virtues: piety, purity, submissiveness, and domesticity." Put them all together and they spell: mother, daughter, sister, wife— WOMAN. With them she is promised happiness and power. This is considered evidence of the male effort to hold females in bondage, like slavery.

Bernadine Healy, M.D., author of *A New Prescription for Women's Health*, stated at a meeting on "New Dimensions in Cardiology," in Dayton, Ohio, that over ten thousand women had written to her stating that their doctors would not listen to them. This could be interpreted as, since they don't own and control land they are not really important. There is a trend for females to use female physicians, because they feel more equal and are listened to better.

In *Megatrends for Women,* Patricia Aburdene and John Naisbitt discuss what they call a "critical mass for social transformation." They describe a vision of full participation of women in society at the highest level of creativity and leadership, from politics, to religion, to the arts, to business. They also describe the integration of female values and thought into institutions from the family, to sports, to spirituality; and the shaping of a genuine New World Order, where positive traits of women and men fuse into a new partnership, that are reflected into a making of social structures and a subsequent government. All of this new attitude simply means joining in with man to vie for the territory, to share the HAT syndrome.

A landmark step in women's liberation, little noticed now, was the United States Civil Rights Act of 1957. It was aimed at minimizing the problems of black minorities at that time, but it also entitled millions of females (of all races) to a step up the territorial ladder.

A discussion which caught the imagination of the working female, was the Anita Hill/Clarence Thomas U.S. Senate hearing. This television-aired hearing of a female accusing a prospective Supreme Court appointee of sexual misconduct showcased territorial policy and administrative males trying to decrease female access. It ended by awakening the wrath of females. (There were no females on the hearing committee.)

Although Ms. Hill did not prevail in her televised appearance to block a Supreme Court nominee, she caught the admiration of female watchers and was rewarded by speaking tours and a special professorship at her teaching institution, the University of Oklahoma in Norman.

Many of these incidents opened up pathways to sexual equality in a relationship never before imagined, allowing a share in the "X" syndrome: jobs, food, money. This is an opening for the process of equalization of female-male opportunity—for females and males to vie for the ultimate prize: territory.

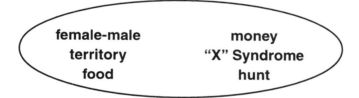

Women have traditionally been directed by centuries of culture, and some anatomical differences reflecting "women virtues," so that there is structured feminist activity slanting toward continuing the "good woman syndrome," adhering to traditional values. When a male is born, his father proudly envisions superficially-covered territory activities, wraps him in blue blankets, and gives him contest toys. Female children, in their pink blankets, have dolls and pretend household duties thrust at them, to divorce them from land control. Some women feel that the bearing and raising of children alone should bring equal status and recognition with the hunting, land-holding male, but this is no equation. There is progress to a time when females in the United States can play territorially on a level field.

Remember About Skin

Three

RACE
REMEMBER ABOUT SKIN

THE FOUR YEAR OLD GIRL LEAFED THROUGH THE BIG AL-phabet book. I explained the pictures as we turned the pages, "A is for apple. Remember that you can eat it! B is for ball. Remember that you can bounce it! C is for cat. Remember that you can play with it!"

Suddenly, the little girl stopped me and asked, "Daddy, why are some people different colors than other people?"

"Well," I explained, "some people are different colors, but under their skin they are all the same."

The inquisitive four year old looked up; "So the thing to remember about skin is to have some!"

*   *   *   *

Many times in group discussions, with both white and black communities or other ethnic groups, it is obvious that the discussion is on a superficial and emotional level, with no real knowledge of the depth of the problem involved. Representative groups of the establishment, concerned with the problems of the United States, are motivated by subconscious impulses not seen on the surface. Rational discussion fails to bring about desired ends and it is obvious that most, if not all, of the power structure is not interested or active in any real participation toward an equalization of status.

It seems necessary to revise the whole approach to see if there is something involved in race relations that is not obvious. To begin, one must try to identify the problem of racism. I find if one tries to identify racism, it becomes a nebulous thing, only characterized in general terms, and is not really responsible for social exchange and racial interaction.

It is apparent that there must have previously been some environmental influence at work (not specifically recognized), which might point the way to action by groups or individuals in racial confrontation. In general, examination of psychiatric principles fails to reveal definite evidence of any known factor that could influence racial interaction. The behavioral sciences are replete with ideas of animals seeming to react to territorial bounds with definite predictability. It is as if they were DNA-programmed in a certain way. Applications of this pattern brings the apparent conclusion that animals express territorialism without definite thinking processes. We know there isn't any reason to believe that man's ability to rationalize, communicate, and have opposing finger dexterity, removes him from this territorial programming. From this viewpoint, if we then look at racial problems, we find that man's actions can be forecast and explained, almost without exception, if they are related to territory. This can be used to make regional confrontation understandable and allow us to manipulate our social problems on a local, state, or national level.

Consider fundamental historical principles involving racial problems. It is thought that man's everyday performance will total his heredity and environment. Although there are many variations of this rationalization, most authorities agree on this general line of thought.

In 1927, Freud first divided personality into the id, the ego, and the super-ego. He structured the personality by relating repression and the dynamic unconscious. The inner play between these voices and the environment resulted, according to Freud, in the behavior of the individual. Carl Jung thought psychic activity included personal conscious and unconscious, and collective unconscious. The personal unconscious involved forgotten memories and unconscious learning. The collective unconscious, he thought, was the most significant—a heritage of the ancestral experience of man that contains the distillate of primitive human experience, which by natural selection has served the human species through the ages. Today we might call this genetic memory.

Adolph Meyer, who is sometimes referred to as the father of American Psychiatry, maintained that multiple factors were important in the mystery of normal and abnormal behavior. He thought personality was the more or less adaptive integration of the biologic organism. Henry Stack Sullivan felt that instincts are used, and we are taught to use them, rather than patterns of behavior being biologically determined. One of Erich Fromm's basic theories is that acculturation is the major human motivational factor.

Many authorities have advanced the notion that most hereditary influence is animalistic and territorialistic.

We might consider that racial problems are significant group reactions. We can note that when man is first born, the world presents a very difficult place. Man soon realized that he was no match for his natural enemies. For his own protection, and to ease his fears, he banded with persons of like characteristics to protect himself against fearful beings, real or imagined. This way he might have developed his own social group—his own status, a caste-like system into which he welcomes individuals with characteristics similar to his, and repels those who threaten to invade his group. A perceived invader could then be repelled individually within the group, or ousted by the entire group.

If we continue this line of thought, we can envision a social complex as being a vast number interacting in small social groups, all of which have some main or common characteristics, which include members of other groups or other circles. We must then face the fact that in racial problems, a group reaction must always seem to be related to territory. At every step of the cultural level—in recreation, work, wage level, and many other overlapping areas, there seems to be a bond to territory.

If we speak of racial prejudice as being environmental, or if we speak of the rightness or wrongness of racism, we have just scratched the surface to group or territorial relationships. Any interpretation of racial prejudice or discrimination, based on rightness or wrongness as far as morals are concerned, presents a problem. As a conscious approach to group or territorial relationships, there are too many interactions and influences on our basic personality necessary for man to follow a course suggested on the basis of idealism.

Fromm wrote that social factors affect psychopathology more than biological factors, and that man and society interact dynamically. Fromm also states that man's most compelling problem has to do with the need that society has created in him and that man slaves for fame, power, love, and a realization of humanistic and religious ideals. I am proposing further that Man, propelled by still un-isolated plasmids or chromosomes, makes man's most compelling problem land control.

A religious approach to racism has been markedly limited in effect. The problem with this viewpoint is that many religious denominational tendencies exist, and not all of them try to rigidly adhere to a problem approach. At the same time, each of these religions has its own variations and problems. For that reason, concentrated efforts to make a unified religious approach to racial problems are not significant enough for most religious power structures to warrant risk of internal strife or rejection. It is simply too fraught with emotion to become a major religious issue.

There is no major moral or ethnic difference clearly and concisely related to the situation. There is no common religious factor. Habits, likes and dislikes, economic situations, living conditions, race, and education all work to neatly place persons in a specific class group. Once placed in a class group, however, it is obvious that territorialism is the final key.

At an annual meeting of the American Association for the Advancement of Science in February 1995, Luca Caralli-Sforza, a Stanford University population geneticist, stated that races are "not different when we look under the skin." He had previously stated "no documented biological superiority of any race, however defined."

Judging from many studies, we can discard the question of equality or non-equality of physical or mental characteristics.

A strong genetic basis, which can be attributed to animalistic territorial responses in man, can be called the HAT syndrome—Human Animal Territorial Syndrome—a carry-over from evolutionary man. We continuously observe birds flying south in the winter, returning thousands of miles the following spring to the same yard, trees, and general area. An invasion of this area by strange birds of the same species immediately evokes an attack-defense reaction by the regular territorial inhabitants. The same thing is true of the ape-gorilla-chimpanzee family. While they range over a wild area as a group, they do not go beyond definite limits. Within these limit they have territorial feeding grounds, territorial play grounds and territorial sleeping grounds. Likewise, they repel invaders of their area by aggressive displays, even though they may be outnumbered or disadvantaged.

We can extend an analogy to the lion and his cat family down through the animal kingdom. In this instance, we are all lions. Without dwelling further on this phenomenon in the animal world, it is easy to see a real application to man. Villages compete against villages, cities against cities, states against states, and countries against countries, even when boundaries are not natural, such as rivers or mountains, etc.

On the basis of speech, habit, color, religion, and so forth, an invasion of territorial areas quickly evokes a fight. In some cases, color is a part of Identification Manifestation. An illustration quickly comes to mind. Some time ago, a black student from the University of Cincinnati Conservatory of Music was sent to a racially segregated southern area to teach in an all-white high school. While she was there, she taught in the school, lived with a white family, participated within the social structure, and finally returned to her home base. Because of her very light skin color, she was never identified as being black; and her speech, habits, religion, and scholastic background, identified her as part of the territory. She had no problems. As American blacks are increasingly gaining a financial and social base, this might not be unusual, but the illustration stands.

A common result of transplanting animals or man to a new area is that the new areas are staked out and defended. Examples of this would be the colonization of North America and the emergence of Canada, the United States, Australia, India, and South Africa from British rule. Even the settlement of Israel fits this pattern of newcomers quickly adopting an attack-defense territorial pattern. The new nation is fiercely, militarily defended.

On a smaller scale, this is essentially what has happened in present so-called racial confrontations in the United States. In Los Angeles, black families confined to ghetto areas by forced economic rule for over two hundred years finally staked out territory to repel white invaders by burning and looting even inanimate reminders of their crowding: buildings, stores, autos driving through, and apartments (all of which were owned by white invaders). Then blacks spoke of having their own banks, stores, businesses, and schools, even though economically they would suffer. They clamored for their own area, exhibiting human animal territorialism. The same activity happened in Sarajevo. Departing Croations burned their loved possessions and houses before leaving, and the new inhabitants will establish their land claim.

It is easy to see how open housing and its fierce resistance is evidently a manifestation of territorialism. Open housing is perceived as an invasion of territory by an outsider, easily identified as belonging to another territory. The occupant's human animal territorialism is evoked, either rationally or irrationally from a genetic level, utilizing any means needed to repel the territorial invader.

Remotely on a personal basis, I saw an area in which I would like to build a house that had a "For Sale" sign prominently displayed. I called the real estate office and was told the manager would be right over to show me the land, but when he came, I was standing in the doorway of my office. He looked surprised and drove away. After some time passed, I was told that the manager had an accident and had been taken to a hospital. After several days, I called again, and was then told in a laughing manner that he had moved to Florida and the land was not available. The land was then sold to a white physician. Still, however, this racial incident was not really racial in basis. I was identified as someone from another territory. With increased monetary leverage of some blacks today, especially athletes, this might not happen in most areas.

We have had many riots in the United States in the last several years, but even a superficial scanning of the situation reveals that these were in definite areas. All were confined into manifestly identifiable, mostly suppressed territories, and represented the revolt of the inhabitants of the territory against outsiders.

The largest riot of all began in Los Angeles on April

29, 1992, with 55 deaths, 1,980 injuries, 4,591 fires, and almost 12,000 arrests, and approximate insured losses approaching one billion dollars. Over 4,500 Army and Marine troops were ordered to the city; while 3,200 National Guard troops were held in reserve. It all began when a video tape of a black person representing a minority territory, being beaten by white policemen representing a different territory, was televised. The situation seemed so explicit and understandable that the minority territory believed that the offending territory invaders would be adequately punished. When they were not, the police force found not guilty, the minority territory (comprised mostly of blacks, some Hispanics and some whites) revolted; destroying and burning anything that appeared representative of outside territorial influence.

Racial incidents like this are still happening. In October 1996, a black motorist was killed by a white policeman in St. Petersburg, Florida, which set off rioting that left 28 buildings burned and 11 people injured, including a police officer who was shot. Scores of extra police patrolled the streets and the Florida National Guard was called to the area.

This is human territorialism at its simplest. For some, it has been hard to understand why persons would burn down what would seem to be their own houses, would loot what seems to be their own stores, would shoot at and turn over automobiles of persons passing through the area. For some, it has been difficult to understand that these stores actually represent the outside territory because they were owned by persons outside of the area in which the disturbance took place. The apartments and houses burned were symbolic of the outside territorial invaders—the owners were living in other neighborhoods or in other areas of the town or city. The automobiles were driven by persons identifiable by their racial features as being from outside the territory. Essentially normal individuals, holding good job situations, were involved, persons who did not necessarily need the looted material: appliances, television sets, clothing, and other things. This was a manifestation of the HAT syndrome at work.

In contrast, after the January 17, 1994, earthquake in California—with losses estimated in the billions of dollars—looting was virtually non-existent. All territorial inhabitants were equally affected.

On college campuses, we have seen college students band together and riot, to gain more acceptance of black identity—either when they were allowed to or of their own volition.

Occasionally, these students wanted black professors and asked for their own buildings in which they could have their own programs and their own control. Such buildings, like the one given to Antioch University students in Yellow Springs, Ohio, in the 1970's and named "Imoja," did not allow white janitors, white maids, or any other whites to come inside. That was black territory, and the badge of the invaders from the outside happened to be color: white racial coloration.

The situation did not persist, however, because the black students within six months found when they excluded themselves and set up their own area, they lost advantages of the University quickly, and were perceived as not being part of the University. They reversed the situation and the one hundred and thirty-one students who started the black dormitory started slipping back into the Antioch University structure, where the students were perceived as belonging to the University again. When the dormitory census finally dropped to thirteen, the school closed it.

Some black leaders talk of having control over their own communities, over their own banks, and their own stores. They speak of eventually having their own state as the ultimate in control.

This misguided effort of separation quickly denies separatists from participating in the whole unit structure of governmental activity, even though to some it would seem to have temporary advantages in strong spot participation, such as a Black Caucus or Muslim religious order. If separatism goes to the extreme, then there is denial of the advantage of group participation.

If we may project this thought further, open housing is a necessity for a working democracy. It is absolutely necessary for inhabitants to think that their territory consists of a wide area, not the restricted region in which they have been forced to live over long periods of time by outside territorial inhabitants.

An adequate approach to the riot-torn and devastated area in Los Angeles was not to rebuild the area, but to adequately make available projects to disperse and allow these inhabitants to move into and be a functioning part of the whole Los Angeles tract, rather than to reconstruct their old territorial base. Reconstruction of the riot-torn area is really a rejection of democratic principles and will result in even more separatism.

Black economist Glenn C. Loury has been quoted as making a strong case for the re-discovery of black racial honor, and American courts and schools are debating ending school integration, a terrible prospect for all minorities.

As for education's swing toward separate schools, Kenneth Clark, a sociologist, is quoted, "Talk about separate but equal, if they are going to be equal, why are they separate?"

It is absolutely necessary that territorialism and its

manifestation should be a matter of concern for a power structure wishing to consider racial problems. No meaningful approach to racism can be made unless this syndrome is clearly understood, whether it is called Human Animal Territorialism or some other name. It is necessary that we be aware of this as one of the basic underlying problems involved in our cities and towns, in our causes, in our international action, and in man's reactions for the foreseeable future; especially in the whole world approach our communications and computers have opened.

The use of the term "racism" has limited descriptive power. The time has come to use terminology that may be computer-oriented, community-descriptive, and discussion-understandable. "T-Factor," meets all of these parameters. All races and cultures regard their land of origin with fondness, but must realize their present circumstance is a part of an ongoing social structure.

I might illustrate how national organizations, such as the United States Urban League and the National Association For the Advancement of Colored People (NAACP), could visualize a territorial approach in their quest for racial harmony and progress. They should fight for the "American" way not for "Afro-Americans." The territorial projection should be: American-Afros, American-Hispanics, American-Orientals, and American Disenfranchised Minorities. Then the Urban League and NAACP could position themselves to:

1) Press American Blacks to pursue education
2) Press American Blacks to organize business
3) Press American Blacks to be politically active
4) Press American Blacks to be job-oriented
5) Press American Blacks to be functionally and visibly a part of the "American Way."

Their projections should be inclusive of all minorities.

With interactive virtual reality, they could have involvement with major video manufacturers to provide expertise, suggestion, and design for working social modules. Interactive video could be aimed at determining racial attitude of public service employees and executives, with interactive games programming social dimensions.

Leading purveyors and designers of interactive video games, such as Panasonic, Atari, Sega, or Sport Games could easily work out interactive social programming that would quantitate and define racial progress and community problems along lines of more harmony, and social and business interaction.

CHRISTIANITY

Latin Cross

HINDUISM

Shiva

JUDAISM

Star of David

ISLAM

Star and Crescent

CONFUCIANISM

Confucius

BUDDHISM

Buddha

SHINTO

Torii

TAOISM

Yin-Yang

Religion

Four

PRAYER
WHAT'S RELIGION GOT TO DO WITH IT?

IT WAS ONE HUNDRED AND TWENTY DEGREES IN THE shade—and there was no shade. I left the hotel in Calcutta and walked down the street, my uniform soaked with sweat. I entered the bazaar, where there were rows of stalls. I approached the second stall, with hanging food and bread covered with flies. A small Indian girl, ragged, dirty, and covered with angry sores, was holding a thin, crying child. She held out her hands and cried, "Bakshees, Sahib, bakshees!" I gave her two anna, worth nearly two cents, years ago.

Three or four stalls down, three native boys approached me. "Bakshees, Sahib! No mother. No father.

No sister. No brother. Bakshees, Sahib!" I spread several more anna around, and before I moved a few steps, I had thirty or forty begging women and children around me crying, "Bakshees, Sahib! No mother. No father. No sister. No brother. Bakshees, Sahib!" I realized word had spread that there was a stupid guy in a uniform passing money around.

"Jaldi hi. Jaldi hi!" (Go away. Go away!) I yelled. I then waved my hands and they disappeared.

In the doorway of a shop, I spotted a well-dressed Indian, obviously the owner. He stood, leaning against the wall, watching me. "You saw what happened here," I said. "What do you do? How do you handle these people?"

He replied, "I give one hundred anna a year to the poor."

"That's less than two dollars," I said. "Is that all you do?"

"Sahib," he responded, "every man to his own conscience, every man to his own religion." He nodded and stepped back into his store.

* * * *

By far, the majority of the living species of man believe in some sort of religion, and most religions think of survival beyond our bodily deaths. If one thinks of the continued passage of the genetic strand, the DNA from one body to another, certainly there is survival. In man, there probably is a connection between all of man's living species. If we can grasp the concept of survival by perpetuating the genetic strand, there is also the probability that the same genetic strand that carries life must carry a constancy for the acquisition of territory. It is only that our sense extension is not specific enough to find it yet. Now we find planets by spectrometer and gravitational pull before telescopic intervention. We will certainly find with all the evidence chromosomal programing for territorial acquisition.

It may be that religion is a sham to acquire territory within a territory. A simple example would be the Branch Davidian religious cult in Waco, Texas, whose compound was destroyed by fire in April, 1993. These people had retired from the community, setting up their own living, sleeping, eating, and worshiping quarters.

Let's look at three of the major religions: Christianity, Judaism, and Islam.

Christianity

This is an effort to summarize Christianity into two or three pages and also to illustrate that Christianity, with other religions, is really a kind of territorialism. Christianity is replete with territorial excursions and acquisitions. Briefly, this religion, currently the world's largest, according to available history, began after Jesus Christ, the father of the Christian faith, preached about the Kingdom of God in Palestine. His followers were divided into twelve disciples, called apostles, who spread his word. Jesus insisted upon humility toward God and justice toward men, mercy and brotherhood of man, and love of God for all creatures. Roman authorities thought that Jesus came or wanted to be the king of the Jews, and that he was to lead an uprising against Roman rule in the Palestines. They felt his claim to be threatening, and an act of treason against their state; so Jesus was tried, condemned to death, and crucified.

On the first Easter after the crucifixion, some of the disciples reported Jesus was alive (the resurrection). They claimed Jesus remained on earth for forty days, and then ascended into Heaven.

According to some Christians, the church began fifty days later. The disciples began reporting that the Holy Spirit had entered them. At Antioch, Syria, a community outside of Palestine, these Jewish believers gradually gave themselves the name "Christians." The Romans persecuted the Christians for many years, until an edict by Constantine in the Ecumenical land in 313 A.D. gave them freedom of religion. Christianity then became the official religion of the Roman Empire, about 380 A.D., after the canonization of the New Testament, approximately 367 A.D. The Christians followed two manuals, the Old Testament, and writings which became the New Testament. Christianity developed great economic and political power and held much territory.

The church made many conquests after the year 1000 A.D., with the fall of Constantinople in 1453 A.D. The Crusades began in 1096 A.D., and proceeded on to 1272 A.D., ending in an unsuccessful campaign to retake their Holy Land by the European nations. Tuesday, November 27, 1095, in a field just outside of the walls of the French city of Clermont Ferrand, Pope Urban II preached a sermon. The Pope outlined a plan for a crusade, and called on his listeners to join ranks. Their response was positive and overwhelming. The Pope commissioned the bishops at the council to enlist others to outline a strategy, with individual groups of crusades to begin the journey. Each group would make its way to Constantinople, the Byzantine capital, where, with the Byzantine emperor and his army, they would counter attack against the Seljuk, conquerors of Anatolia. Then the crusaders would campaign against the Muslims in Syria and Palestine, with Jerusalem as their ultimate goal.

In late summer 1096, five major armies set out on the crusade. A majority were from France, others from Lorraine, Burgundy, Flanders, and southern Italy. Only a few survived the journey, reaching Jerusalem on July 15, 1099. Most of this was recaptured by Muslims, and a second crusade was launched in 1145, with disastrous results. The third crusade captured Palestine, but was unable to recapture Jerusalem. The fourth plundered Constantinople, and the last major crusade, organized by King Louis IX, in 1270 was unenthusiastic. The crusades were essentially a religious, political territorial exercise.

Rome fell in 1476 A.D. and the center of the empire shifted to Constantinople, with a rise of Islamic religion. From 1500 A.D. to the present time, the reformation of the Church and the formation of various denominations spread the Church through England, Italy, Bohemia, Northern Germany, Scandinavia, Switzerland, the Netherlands, and Scotland. In 1500 A.D., Protestants broke away from the Catholic Church. Henry VIII, king of England in 1534 A.D., declared the Church of England to be free from the Pope; and a Baptist Church begun in Amsterdam, Holland, spread to Providence, in Newport, in 1639 A.D., with a split off of Friends and Quakers.

"The Thirty Year War," from 1618 A.D. to 1640 A.D., was a larger war between Protestants and Catholics. Christianity continued to spread with exploration and conquests by Spanish, Portuguese, Dutch, French, and English; even entering China and South India, Burma, Sumatra, Hawaii, and Africa. In order to clarify areas that stretched lines of effect, organizations of Ecumenical movement were begun in the 1880's and continued to present time, with meetings and organizations to define these areas.

Certainly all this resulted in and from an attachment to territory. Christian holdings of most territories in the Middle Ages continued to invite suspicion and questions of church versus state. Even today, territorial church acquisitions are still subject to different laws, different taxation, and priorities of regulations of taxes, law enforcement, fire protection, and other services in states and countries: in order to protect ruling agents from territorial seeking religions. In Rome today, there exists Vatican City, an area of rule by Catholics with its own tax base, military and police force, fire department, and even its own money; and is not subject to the laws of its territorial presence: Italy.

It is this author's interpretation that from the time of the Christians at Antioch, through the crusades and the religious spread by conquests of great nations, the basis was control of territory entwined with church. Even taking land away from native Americans was under the guise of religion.

Judaism

From many sources, it is thought that Abraham, historically, was the founder of the Jewish religion. His son, Isaac, and grandson, Jacob, in turn had twelve sons; possibly forming twelve tribes. Jacob, again from different sources, with his tribes and others, lived in Egypt around 1200 to 1700 B.C., and was often in slavery. Moses, around 1300 B.C., with his family of approximately seventy men, plus women, led his followers out of Egypt looking for a geographical area of their own. They finally conquered the land now known as modern Israel. Saul, David, and Solomon tied Israel together; but after Solomon's death, there were northern and southern kingdoms, ending with the conquering of the north by the south.

When Babylon conquered Judea, there was a long period of Jewish dispersal; with Rome barring the Jews from Jerusalem, and scattering the Jews throughout the known world at that time. Simply spoken, Jewish religion was organized in a manner which kept them territorially motivated. Some literature notes that at least ten men were necessary in order to continue prayers. Kosher food, of course, was required. In any religious qualification of marriage, a Jew must marry another Jew, and children are only Jewish if the mother is Jewish. The females had a principle of a washroom together, required for safety. Jewish people set up their own temples in otherwise different cultural areas; but, on the other hand, kept themselves isolated from efficient cultural assimilation.

After World War II there were some questions as to what could be done with misplaced Jews, and what to do with the Jewish population secondary to the war situation. A meeting between Churchill, Stalin, and Roosevelt decided first on Tripoli (objected to by France), and then returned them to the old area of Israel, occupied mostly by Palestinians, and the involved nations helped the Jewish people resettle. Jewish people have been supported by other countries, and have improved both the land and manufacturing there to this day, with the definition and growth of a new state called Israel.

As Israel developed, all of the genetic mechanisms have surfaced, and Israel is a great state, with the boundary guarding effects of genetic programming of territory. In spite of considerable external financing, there is a rejection of outside influence, suspicion, and a rejection of external manipulation and demand for its own decision making like the United Kingdom, United States, Australia, Brazil, etc.

There is continued territorial military action between the Jews and the Palestines, thinly disguised as a religious conflict, though in reality, again, a chromosomal territorial manifestation.

Islam

From a number of sources, Islam is the religion taught by the prophet Mohammed in the 600's A.D., beginning in Mecca. He taught that there is only one God, Allah, and Mohammed (Muhammad) was Allah's messenger. In other words, the three major religions all had great leaders and teachers. Islam covered the Middle East, North Africa, Pakistan, Indonesia, parts of Yugoslavia, Albania, and Turkey. There is a record of Mohammed's flight to Medina, returning to Mecca in 630 A.D. and occupying the city, after which the Meccans accepted Islam and recognized Mohammed as a prophet. The Islamic religion, like others, was laced with territorial acquisitions, beginning with founder Muhammad (570-652), through his war with Mecca and his message, the Koran; and through descendent Askia Mahammad, who transformed an African state into an Islamic Kingdom. Other descendants conquered Constantinople, Greece, Serbia, Bosnia, Albania (later affecting Spain), Portugal, and parts of England. Basically, Muslims regard religion and politics as the same.

Islam spread throughout the Middle East and North Africa, from Northern Spain and stretched to India. From the Koran and Hadith, Islamic Sharia (law) was developed to solve problems of the territories. Many wars were fought between the Christians and Muslims, the most famous being the Crusades, in reference to territorial prerogatives. The jihad, a basic practice, is a belief that it is the duty of every Muslim to share in the military defense of Islam and Muslim territory. HAT is at work here.

All teachings are assembled in the holy Muslim book called the Koran, an Arabic word meaning "the reading." The Koran teaches patience, kindness, honesty, industry, honor, courage and generosity. It permits slavery, but allows slaves to earn freedom, to ask for transfer to other masters, and forbids the splitting of families.

There is history quoted about that period in the Old Testament, and this religion also followed basic moves of territorial acquisition. Structured missionary work and battles were calculated to acquire and spread the Islamic word to Europe, America, Asia, and Africa.

In summation, the great religions of the world function almost as great nations; extending lines of influence and territorial acquisition as they proceed to add converts, which in turn relate to the land; more or less a territorial grab from the persons already living there. All of this follows territorial rules.

Karen Armstrong, writing in her book, *The History of God*, states that religion is highly pragmatic, and that it is far more important for a particular idea of God to work, than for it to be logically or scientifically sound. This is the pattern of religion, to obtain territory primarily, secondarily when government rulers will not allow. This covers the real principle of controlling land for hunting, living, mating, play, and work.

There is a continued pattern of the HAT principle throughout religions. All of us remember the story of Moses leading the Israelites out of Egypt to the Promised Land; and the Puritans, who separated from the church of England, and settled in the colony of Plymouth, in New England.

Joseph Smith, along with other associates, founded the Church of Jesus Christ of Latter-day Saints in New York in 1830, commonly called the Mormon religion, with many splinter groups moving to Ohio, Missouri, Illinois, and finally the main body settling in the valley of the Great Salt Lake (Utah) in 1847. There they built temples, meeting houses, chapels, houses of worship, cathedrals, and recreation halls.

In Rome lies Vatican City, an independent country consented to by the Italian government in 1929. It houses the government of the Catholic Church. It has its own water, lighting, telephone, and street cleaning systems; and also its own flag, stamps, and coins. Vatican City is noted for its library and Cathedral, St. Peters. It is an example of man's propensity for territorialism.

By examining historical facets of various religions, we can see the effect of our genetic chromosomal thrust to take land.

First, there is a group gathering around a leader; then the settling of a place (land) for meeting, a church, a synagogue, or a mosque; then extension of territory; and finally, the extension of that territory—Judaism from Egypt to Palestine; Moslem throughout Europe, Spain, Portugal, France, and into England; Catholic into the colonies. Everywhere the new, more powerful religion surfaced, it destroyed the local religion, attached to the area, and established new religious ruling guidelines.

An example still continuing is Ireland, about which thousands of papers, articles, and books have been published. England handled it like their other colonies in that time frame. They conquered the land from Irish Catholics; turned the land over to Protestant settlers to colonize and rule; and making, on occasion, rules against Irish holding land and other rules of status. Thousands of deaths, really murders, have occurred since the war officially ended, supposedly in the name of religion, and continue all of this is in the English tradition of that time, operating in all its colonies.

In 1972, Clive Limpkin wrote about Ulster in *The Battle of Bogside*. "The Catholics," he said, "are blacks who happen to have white faces. Like the poor whites of America who persecute the blacks, it is the poor Catholic who suffers at the hands of his Protestant counterpart." Elsewhere in his writing, he calls the conflict a colonial war.

He summed up his observation this way: "The Protestant feels so British, enjoying all the benefits of British citizenship, that he is willing to fight and die, rather than be ruled by a foreign government, an emotion shared by the Catholic, who feels he already is being ruled by a foreign government." Territorial attachment to religion is clear.

War

Five

Your Land, My Land
Tossed Salad Effect

"America is God's crucible, the great melting pot where all the races of Europe are melting and re-forming!"

This phrase originated in the "Melting Pot," a turn-of-the-century (1908) play by Israel Zangwill. It was later enlarged by Thomas E. Dewey, who told reporter John Jaunther in 1947, "New York City is not a melting pot, it's a boiling pot."

In 1979, at a meeting in New York, Dr. Frederick Kao said, "When I came to this country, I expected to find a melting pot. But, no, it is a tossed salad—with bits and pieces of different cultures swirling around."

In 1974, at Central State University in Ohio, President Lionel Newsome fumed that the total tornado destruction of the University was not reported until two days later by the Xenia paper, only three miles away. The answer was clear. The black university had isolated itself from the area—the tossed salad effect, seeking black identity. Since it was isolated, there was decreased awareness about this settlement, only a few miles away. It still is not perceived as being a part of the area.

*   *   *   *

Territories are usually areas in which most animals (in our example) hunt, eat, play, or socialize. Dr. Peter Marsh, writing in *Eye to Eye*, noted that individuals dispersed with available food need little territorial defense, if the population is small and food is plentiful; but with scarce food, stricter territories are established to force out some animals. He felt that space control in humans is much more complex and helps to set the scene for social interaction, lists primary homes, territory rites and rituals, "home field" advantages, shared territories, and temporary territories.

Sandra Gardner, writing in *Street Gangs in America*, felt that young people in poor urban areas get involved in gangs because gangs are an innate part of the neighborhood, culture, family, or all three; but felt that the needs of young people in neighborhood or culture are not being met. She named a multiple program approach in Seattle, Boston, and Los Angeles. She named new ingredients—lack of jobs, increase in poverty, and the proliferation of drugs and violence, as a part of the gang problem.

Jesse Jackson, in a California speech, asked blacks to reclaim their territory from crime, to cooperate with police, and to report criminal action. *Defensible Space,* written by Oscar Newman in 1972, tries to show by illustration and design that crime prevention, through definitive urban design planning, could be implemented in housing complexes and apartments.

In *Coping with Weapons and Violence,* Maryann Miller discussed the current state of school violence, compared Canadian gun control (Rifles: a certificate, passive training, reference, interview of associates, and a twenty-eight day delay. Handguns: limited fire power, and special registration for specific purposes.) She felt this contributed to a considerable reduction in violent crimes.

She noted articles in reference to poverty, easy gun access, and drugs. She quoted Charles Silbermen, who wrote in *Criminal Violence—Criminal Justice,* that violent crime will not be eliminated until every person in America becomes a full participating member of society, with a major stake in its preservation. She wrote of multiple programs: the California Conservation Corps, with varieties which have now extended to twelve states; and Lincoln Hall, a residential treatment facility program with centers in Dallas, Houston, and San Antonio. All of these fairly successful programs, it would seem, would educate youths to realize that they are a part of the territory and, thus, have options open to them other than crime.

A review of literature regarding city, and now national gangs, solidly links gangs to a territorial base. Sociologist Carl S. Taylor, conducting a study of Detroit gangs, divided them into scavenger gangs, territorial gangs, and corporate gangs. He noted all gangs link control of a specific area or neighborhood to ethnic or some other easily-identified territorial manifestation. This can be racial, cultural, or activity-related.

Perhaps, as manufacturing and job options move from manual labor to computer technology, leaving millions of disenfranchised youths, a special emphasis must be placed on training for them, or their basic genotype drive will progress into more violent behavior, abetted by a lenient court system, and an inability to have territorial significance.

The problems with gang activities may simply be competition for available resources, where the population is under-served and under-capitalized. In *Behavioral Ecology,* Manfred Milenski and Geoffrey A. Parker felt that if there is spatial distribution of resource items in a rich patch, competitors need not interfere with each other. They go on to say that many competitors have a probability of interfering over the same items if resources are limited. That they are discussing avian interference is beside the point. The point is, simply, that where resources are limited—food, housing, funds—competition is so increased in lower income locations that competitors aggressively try to control resources, leading to gang warfare and street crime. In slum areas throughout the U.S., food and housing is now plentiful by reason of governmental support. Money is not, and there is extreme competition. An entrepreneur has to search for the product which will draw sales from those who have little—and drug products will do that. First, they encourage consumption, then drugs demand their own market. If jobs, better housing, schools, and effective community partnership were more available, then crime would drop as other available options surfaced. The answer, of course, is a more effective distribution of resources.

Values have little part in this. Former U.S. President Jimmy Carter, in a public television interview on May 24, 1994, said, "The discussion of values is most often among people who have everything they want in life." He referred to food, housing, and jobs.

It may be that our United States legal system has roots which reflect our great resources. In the United States, penal system funding is supported, justice is slow, sentences are light or non-existent, and convicts are pampered by resource based conditions: food, medical care, social activities, climate control (heat and air conditioning), television, radio, and around-the-clock guarding.

In other countries, where resources are limited, this is impossible. Because resources to sustain prisoners are in short supply, justice and punishment is swift, and the convicted are quickly returned to society or disposed of in a way not using scarce resources, such as lashing, low-cost confinement, or execution.

The United States is sliding toward enclaves. On the west coast and in Florida the heavy influx of Hispanics has resulted in areas of transplanted ideas and language. Most large cities have large black-oriented sections. Recently, there was reported a third large Chinese neighborhood development in New York. It is interesting that in Canada, persons refer to themselves as Canadians first, then on occasion add national or geographical origin. There are no Afro-Canadians. French speaking inhabitants of Quebec are going through the routine of land attachment, and talk of being "citizens of Quebec."

Unfortunately there has recently surfaced considerable reaction to affirmative action accommodation for minorities, females, and immigrants. Some ill-advised and politically or fiscally-motivated individuals are now advocating defeat of integrating mechanisms in their own interests. This will result in more division, with horrible effects on the less affluent, and minority populations.

Areas of increased national emphasis toward immigrant heritage will increase islets of self rule, with demands by nationality groups for recognition, privileges, and vested interests. It would be far better for a democracy if we were to blend into a melting pot, rather than to perpetuate this tossed salad pattern.

Six

What To Do & How To Do It

If We Want

At a community social planning committee luncheon, a prominent Jewish department store chain owner took over the conversation, boasting of his financial successes and his vacation. Then he turned to an American Negro and asked, "Why doesn't your race do what we did?"

The response: "As I remember, after World War II, England, Russia, and the United States wondered what to do with Jews. They couldn't send them back to Germany, so they started to send them to North Africa, near

Tripoli. France objected strenuously, so they settled on Palestine, where the government was so weak and the land so arid, no nation really wanted it.

"In the beginning," he continued, "if the Jews had become German Jews instead of Jewish Germans, they would have become part of the territory and never would have been decimated."

There was stunned silence, then quickly the hostess intervened and separated them.

*　*　*　*

Once upon a time, as fairy tales go, we were told that life was a simplistic view of right and wrong, of white and black, of good guys and bad guys, of fixed moral values relating to whatever culture we were in at the moment.

Now we know that we are driven by multiple factors suggested and actuated by basic animalistic factors, shaded by demands of the moment and the culture of the hour.

In the original HAT, I observed an attack defense reaction by the regular territorial inhabitant, an avian observation.

Many observations in the animal kingdom relate to:

1. Territorial feeding ground: for man, the work-ethic set of values actually veil its real meaning; hunting.

2. Territorial play grounds: for man this could be a favorite corner gathering place, to parks, to giant arenas.

3) Territorial sleeping grounds: for man this could be a corner alley, to bedrooms in homes, motels, and hotels, etc.

Invaders are fended off by militant display, even though the inhabitants are outnumbered or disadvantaged. Examples are the successful Vietnamese defense against French and American military troops; the Afghanistan army's successful defense against a huge Russian military action; Somalia's rejection of United Nation's troops; and Bosnia's grudging rejection of troops.

It is easy to discern a real application of territorialism to racial problems, housing problems, and gang warfare. High schools, colleges, and universities compete against each other. Countries compete against other countries, and religions follow territorial rules.

As long ago as 1943, Wendell Willkie, a leading advocate of international cooperation, wrote a best selling book, *One World*, in which he claimed necessary understanding and cooperation among the leaders and people of all nations, without realizing the strength of genetic attachment to land.

I have noted the strong probability that male-female relationship is territorial based. I have considered the race question and discussed a religious approach. It is all symbolic manifestation of territorial programming.

Politics are a clear example of territorialism. Carol M. Swain, author of *Black Interests,* wrote in the December 27, 1993 issue of the *Wall Street Journal*: "The segregation of black voters into black majority districts may produce easy electoral victories for black candidates, and may insulate incumbents from opponents, but it virtually precludes further political gains." She observes that if black candidates mostly run for office in black districts, those who choose to seek statewide office, such as governor, or the U.S. senate, face an added disadvantage of lacking connections to a larger base with needed support, and accumulate little experience in developing and maintaining bi-racial coalitions. She is really saying that political candidates must have support of the territory in order to win.

I propose a "no fault" approach to racial problems, which avoids major confrontations. If we proceed from a basis that we are genetically programmed to take up territory, there is no blame to accept or demand, and procedure can be devised toward desired results. For instance: in the United States, a democratic society, this opens an entire new group of options.

There is probability that territoriality can be measured, and this measure could be used to plan approach. An example would be an agenda relating to racial problems. Suppose that after a racial incident, a community or a police force could examine the incident in reference to territoriality by testing and assigning a score, or a "K" rating. The group involved could then be exposed to psychological or religious programming, or specialists in these fields, and, after reassessment, could be given a new "K" unit test to identify what, if any, of the programming changed set values. Retesting by virtual reality would confirm the value of that approach.

Virtual reality has surfaced, giving a more complete aspect of many problems. Virtual reality has brought new parameters into study of the many aspects of health care, engineering design, architecture, and cyberspace. In military matters, virtual reality uses interactive simulators. Interactive video programs, with decision-making scenarios, now provide us with the next step in educating visualization of problem approach. There is no reason that this cannot be employed to rate individual and group territoriality and change after appropriate intervention. It has been reported that at MIT, Media Laboratory Path Planning (a way to guide a virtual simulation through its environment) and Motor Planning (the behavior of virtual minds) are being used and investigated. Literally and essentially, if we can emulate and mimic happenings in real life in terms of virtual reality, then we can quantify and extrapolate relative social happenings. In an earlier chapter, I noted that we can only think in terms of the science of the moment, and virtual reality is the leading edge of the science of this moment.

Francis Hammid, in *Virtual Reality and the Exploration of Cyberspace*, described human interaction from telegraph operators through radial telephones and cyberspace. Interactive electronic mediation is now essentially accessible to anyone. He described virtual reality as a method allowing people to manipulate information in a

"J" Unit

computer, to enhance ability to deal with the increasingly complex technological society. He spoke of glove and head mount displays, of desktop virtual reality, of the computer monitor or video screen, and cab-style reality, using the same techniques as military flight simulators, extending to include groups of people. The Internet is with us now and is generally available.

This extension of computer-generated space, now over twenty years in observation, may be the entry point in solving predictable human approach to social values.

"J" Unit—Measuring Thought And Reaction

For instance, a major problem in our criminal court procedure is when to recognize that criminals are dangerous to society, when to confine them, and when to pardon them. Judicial boards have to rely on very flimsy information to make judgmental value: jailed conduct, impressions of psychologists and/or psychiatrists, and previous history.

Virtual reality testing could determine probable activity after release, plotted on a "J" scale and available for record keeping, filing, or transference.

At the Ford Motor Company in Dearborn, Michigan, computer experts have created a "virtual town" that you can drive through using a desk top computer mouse. They have held off-site workshops in accounting and

purchasing, and have a vision of seven world-wide design studios linked with computers. Ford calls this virtual "co-location."

The predictive values analysis afforded to us by this approach is the entry point to vast new knowledge, which can both manipulate and advance, or destroy social problems as we know them.

Estimation of territorial projection certainly would be helpful in housing, job competition, crime prevention, estimation of gang activity, and a myriad of other applications. We can play by territorial rules simply observed: for example, a visitor from Germany traveling through the United States deserves respectful treatment. This identifiable visitor, who makes no impact on the HAT in charge of the area (for instance, food supply, resources, or population extension), is generally tolerated. Everyone is outraged when such visitors are assaulted or victimized. An example of that could be the treatment of a student from a competing school on another campus, a northerner in a southern area with auto difficulty, or a visitor from another country assaulted while on vacation.

In an area where literally hundreds of assaults are tolerated as matter of fact, a criminal act involving such a stranger gets wide publicity.

With virtual reality, we can plan what I call "Mobility

of Territorality;" cases where the genetic impulse has to factor in individual perspectives, culture polarizations, common interests, and environmental perspectives. In that way, an assessment can relate to a scene or a pattern.

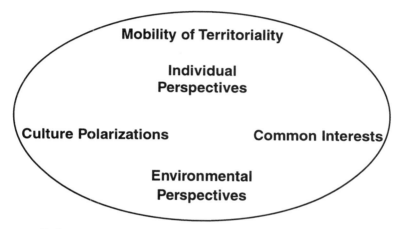

Culture, environment, and social pressures would not factor in a written examination with basic questions, but are possible to interpret with virtual reality. With this in mind, we can finally plan around some social catastrophes present in today's world. With virtual reality, there seems a chance to accomplish what was so lucid many years ago, when I was thinking in terms of rating human animal territorialism on a "J" scale. At that time, the thought was to set up questionnaires relating to concept, but proved too complex to guarantee reproducible results. Now, in an investigation at Loma Linda University Medical Center, David Warner was quoted as saying, "We are quantifying human performance."

It is time to discard the term "racism" as a working module. It is archaic and obsolete. It is not definable— qualitatively or quantitatively. There is no way it can be used for comparison. I suggest "T-Factor" for its replacement. "T- Factor" indicates depth, purpose, and extension of racial or other problems. It allows geographical comparison and computer extension.

What are the desired results of analytical virtual reality in humans? Unfortunately, human animal territoriality has no moral or religious value. Therefore, it can be programmed or allowed to be perceived or manipulated by those in power. Imagine if you can, nations paying only lip service to moral obligations, which of course has happened throughout eternity under thin veneer, Human Animal Territorialism.

All races, societies, religions, and countries have murdered, raped, and pillaged. None are above reproach. All are "Human Animal Territorialism."

It's Kairos time.

EPILOGUE

It has been a long time since Dr. Warren Banner, field representative for the National Urban League, suggested that I write a manual for field workers—a general problem approach, that would relate to all racial situations. The year was 1968.

Twenty-nine years have passed—during which time I wrote "HAT," "Human Animal Territorialism," and "We Are All Lions"; enjoyed a long personal hiatus, which allowed for scientific discovery and interpretation; and experienced the coming of the computer age. Finally, the opportune time to expand on this suggestion has presented itself.

Remarkably, at the core of racial problems is the same factor that programs every other facet of our daily lives. It controls gender relations, religious generalities, and almost all of our life experiences.

Genetic programming to take control of and maintain possession of "turf" extends through every phase of our life. It is instilled at conception, becomes more apparent as we mature, and continues until we die.

Some applications are subtle and not immediately recognized. Following are three recent examples:

- In early 1977, twenty-four North Korean sailors were massacred when their submarine was inadvertently beached in South Korea.

  This accidental invasion of "turf" was met with immediate, hostile reaction.

- Supreme Court Judges Scalia, Kennedy, and Berger emphatically interrupted Attorney General Janet Reno in December 1996, while she was proclaiming her support of a ruling that would allow law enforcement officers to order *all* of the occupants of an automobile, that was stopped for a traffic violation, out of the car.

  At issue here was subconsciously ordering persons out of their own "territory."

- In November 1996, Texaco Corporation agreed to pay females and minorities $176 million to settle court claims of disenfranchised and job exclusion. This led other corporations to follow suit.

This exposed an attempt to exclude competition from accessing occupied "turf."

It is apparent that these occurrences relate to genetic disposition, the human drive to claim and retain land, the basic instinct to remain alive, and the acquisition and protection of territory for support and family extension.

Racial problems are yet another evidence of that life force and drive.

Dr. John Hale, a professor at Meharry Medical College, once said to our class, "You should be able to explain anything in fifteen minutes." Many publications extend simple propositions or explanations into hundreds of pages, ending with detailed indexes—but with no real conclusions.

I have attempted to enable the reader of this book to grasp basic information quickly, and to readily apply some of the explanations contained within to change his/her lifestyle forever.

As the computer century has evolved it has become much easier to explain to observers what was apparent several years ago. For instance, after a long discussion, Tom Smart, a geneticist, employed by a leading genetic engineering company wrote the following:

> I want to thank you for allowing me this opportunity to review *The Kairos Effect* and discuss the publication with you. Your writing raises interesting ques-

tions regarding the role of our genetic programming in determining how we behave. Your central hypothesis that the drive to control land is genetically determined provides an alternative explanation of many human behaviors that are often described in terms of religion and forms of discrimination including racism.

Importantly, *The Kairos Effect* identifies the possibility of using technology such as computer simulation and virtual reality to model and predict how individuals or groups of people might behave in a particular situation based on the underlying hypothesis that we are genetically programmed to strive to control land. As put forth in the book, "This extension of computer generated space, now over 20 years in observation may be the entry point in solving predictable human approach to social values." Your wisdom and drive to explain the roots of various social problems is apparent throughout the book and your "call" to use state-of-the-art technology to model these behaviors so that we may use these tools to create a better world is admirable.

It's my hope that readers can grasp the tremendous impact of this new look at social problems from a genetic background.

GLOSSARY

DNA (Deoxyribonucleic Acid): an extremely long macromolecule that is the main component of chromosomes and is the material that transfers genetic characteristics in all life forms.

HAT (Human Animal Territorialism): man's affinity for terrain.

Identification Manifestation: recognition factor used to distinguish relation to territory.

"J" Scale: measurements of units of thought and reaction, with minimal thought input.

Jenkins Scale: any way of comparably measuring thought to reaction. Used to predict results.

Mobility of Territoriality: modification of territorial values by environment.

Prion: hypothetical infectious particle composed solely of protein and likened to viruses and variods; but having no genetic component.

Scale Unit: a definite amount or quantity of reaction.

Sense Extension: any external extension that increases perception.

T-Factor: the controlling power in a territory. Relationship to terrain by physically occupying territory.

X Syndrome: Access to food, housing and economic survival.

BIBLIOGRAPHY

Abardene, Patricia & Naisbitt, John. *Megatrends for Women*, Villard Books 1992, Megatrends Ltd.2

Adams, Charles J. *Understanding Islam*, World Book Yearbook 1988, World Book, Inc. Scott Fetz.

Alcoch, John. *Animal Behavior-An Evolutionary Approach*, Sinauer Associates, Inc., Sunderland, MA: 1989.

Ardrey, Robert. *The Territorial Imperative*, Atheneum, NY: 1966.

Armstrong, Karen. *A History of God*, Bolzoi Book, Published by Alfred A. Knopf, Inc: 1993.

Bennett, Lerone Jr. *Before the Mayflower*, Johnson Publishing Co.: 1962.

Blumenbach, Johann: *Colliers Encyclopedia*, Vol. 3, p. 523.

Boynton, Robert S. "The Man in the Black Box," *Mirabella Magazine*, October, 1993, Pages 113-116.

Bylinsky, Gene. "A Digital Adam," *Fortune Magazine*, November 1, 1993, Page 123.

Cecil, Russell, M.D. *Textbook of Medicine*, 9th ed., W.B. Saunders Co., Philadelphia, London.

Dobzhansky, Theodosius. *Heredity and the Nature of Man*, Harcourt, Brace and Worlk, Inc., New York: (1964).

D'Souza, Dinesh. *The End of Racism*, The Free Press: 1995.

Donald S. Sills, editor. *International Encyclopedia of Social Science*, Macmillan and Free Press, New York: 1968.

Encyclopedia of Science and Technology, Vol. 1961, McGraw Hill: 1971.

Franklin, John Hope. *From Slavery to Freedom*, Alfred A. Knopf, New York: 1967.

Glass, Bentley. "The Dynamics of Racial Intermixture," An analysis based on the American Negro, American Journal of Human Genetics, Vol. 5: 1953.

Grand, Joanne. *Black Protest*, Fawcett World Library, New York: 1966.

Healy, Bernadine, M.D. *A New Prescription for Women's Health*, Penguin Books: 1995.

Hubbard, Dr. M. *Gay Women: The Misunderstood Majority,* Ward Publishing, 1992.

Impressions of Donald H. Guyton, M.D. and Carl Jenkins, M.D., "Sickle Cell Incidence in Hospital Admissions," Springfield, OH: 1967.

Jenkins, Carl. "HAT," Journal of Human Relations, pp. 162-172, Second Quarter 1969, Central State University, Wilberforce, Ohio, Vol. 17, No. 2.

Jenkins, Carl. "Human Animal Territorialism, Racial Problem Relationship," Forum Associates, Inc: 1973.

Jenkins, Carl. "We Are All Lions! Racial Problems in Five Minutes," Forum Associates, Inc: 1973.

Jenkins, Carl and Charles Shaffer. "Module for Racial Approach," Wittenberg University. Submitted to *Psychology Magazine*, March, 1975.

Jenkins, Carl and Charles Shaffer. "Racial Problems Correlated with Genetic Bio-Chemistry Basis," *World Journal of Psychosynthesis*, Sep.-Oct., 1976.

Johnson, Cecil E. *Contemporary Readings in Behavior*, McGraw Hill: 1970.

Keebler, Jack. "Cyerspaced Out," *Insight Automobile News*, October 25, 1993.

Klein, Lawrence R., Editor. "Monthly Labor Review," May 1971, Bureau of Labor Statistics, U.S. Dept. of Labor, Washington, D.C.

Krebbs, J.R. and Dabies, Ed. *Behavior Ecology-An Evolutionary Approach*, Sinauer Associates, Inc., Sunderland, MA: 1984.

Larson, Bart and Wendell Amstutz. *Youth Violence and Gangs*, National Counseling Resource Center: 1995.

Limpkin, Clive. *The Battle of Bogside*, Penguin Books: 1972.

Lorenz, Konrad Z. *King Solomon's Ring*, Thomas Y. Crowell Co., New York: 1952.

Loury, Glenn C. *One by One From The Inside Out*, The Free Press: 1995.

Marsh, Peter. *Eye to Eye-How People Interact*, Salem House Publishers, Topsfield, Mass.: 1988 (Chapter 2).

McKusick, Victor A. *Human Genetics*, 2nd Edition, Prentice Hall, Englewood Cliffs, New Jersey: 1969.

Mazur, Alan and Leon S. Robertson. *Biology and Social Behavior*, Free Press, New York: 1972.

Mead, Margaret. "Sense and Nonsense About Race," *Redbook Magazine*, September 1969.

Miller, Maryann. *Coping with Weapons and Violence*, Rosen Publishing, New York: 1993.

Morris, Desmond. *The Human Zoo*, McGraw Hill, New York: 1969.

Pierson, Donald. "Race Prejudice as Revealed in the Study of Racial Situations," pp. 663-641, Selection 84, Thomas E. Laswell, John H. Burma, Sidney H. Aronson, Eds. *Life in Society*, Chicago: Scott Foreman and Co. 1969.

Stern, Curt. *Principles of Human Genetics*, 2nd Edition, S.H. Freeman, San Francisco: 1960.

Stien, Jess (Editor in Chief): *Random House Dictionary of the English Language*, p. 946, 1135, Random House, New York, 1966.

Taylor, Ralph. *Human Territorial Functioning*, Cambridge University Press, New York: 1988.

United Nations Bulletin: *Segregation in South Africa*, p. 3, United Nations Publication, Sales No. E. 69. I. 15.

Vogel, F. & Motulsky, A.G. *Human Genetics*, Spring-Verlag Inc: 1986.

Wesley, Charles H. *In Black America 1968*, International Library of Negro Life and History, Publishers Co. New York: 1969

West, Cornel. *Race Matters*, Beacon Press: 1993.

Wiley, Ralph. *What Black People Should Do Now!*, Ballantine Books: October 1993.

Wilson, William Julius. *The Declining Significance of Race*, University Chicago Press: 1980, 2nd Edition.

Wilson, William Julius. *The Truly Disadvantaged, The Inner City, The Underclass, and Public Policy*, University Chicago Press, 1987.

INDEX

ORDER INFORMATION

THE KAIROS EFFECT

If your local bookstore is unable to obtain this
book, you may order it directly from:

Medical Place Publishers
2055-57 South Limestone Street
Springfield, Ohio 45505
Phone: 937-324-5638
937-525-0190
Fax: 937-324-5639

Please send payment of $8.95 for each copy, plus $2.50 for
shipping and handling to the above address. Make check or
money order out to: Medical Place Publishers.

THE KAIROS EFFECT

Cover design by Eric Norton

Text design by Mary Jo Zazueta
in ITC Galliard

Text stock is 60 lb. Windsor Vellum

Printed and bound by McNaughton & Gunn
Saline, Michigan

Production Editor: Alex Moore